Loud, Proud, and Jewish

Loud, Proud, and Jewish

2020 Paperback Edition, *First Printing*
© 2020 by Menachem Creditor
Cover artwork: © 2020 by Ariel Creditor

All rights reserved. No part of this book may be reproduced or transmitted in any form or by means electronic or mechanical, including photocopying, recording, or by any information storage and retrieval system, without permission in writing from the author.

ISBN: 9798602895247

Between stimulus and response there is a space.

In that space is our power to choose our response.

In our response lies our growth and our freedom.

- Viktor Frankl

also by Menachem Creditor

Open to Wonder: Essays (2015-2017)

(*ed.*) None Shall Make Them Afraid

(*ed.*) Holding Fast: Jews Respond to American Gun Violence

(*ed.*) To Banish Darkness: Modern Reflections on Hanukkah

yes, my child: poems

Intense Beginnings: *Selected Writings, 2014*

What Does it Mean? *Selected Writings 2006-2013*

(*ed.*) Not By Might: *Channeling the power of Faith to End Gun Violence*

And Yet We Love: *Poems*

Primal Prayers: *Spiritual Responses to a Real World*

(*ed.*) The Hope: *American Jewish Voices in Support of Israel*

Commanded to Live: *One Rabbi's Reflections on Gun Violence*

Siddur Tov LeHodot: *Shabbat Morning Transliterated Prayerbook*

(*ed.*) Thanksgiving Torah: *Jewish Reflections on an American Holiday*

(*ed.*) A Manifesto for the Future: *Conservative/Masorti Judaism Dreaming from Within*

(*ed.*) Peace in Our Cities: *Rabbis Against Gun Violence*

(*ed.*) Slavery, Freedom, and Everything Between: *The Why, How and What of Passover*

A Pesach Rhyme

Avodah: A Yom Kippur Story

Rabbi Rebecca and the Thanksgiving Leftovers

This book is dedicated to the
professionals and volunteers
of UJA-Federation New York,
who daily give of themselves
to make this world a better, safer,
and more beautiful place.

CONTENTS

9	**Introduction** Rabbi Menachem Creditor
13	**Foreword: This is Our Moment** Melanie Roth Gorelick
17	**Raise up the Joy** Rabbi Annie Tucker
26	**My Mom Used to Say** Ruth Zakarin
32	**How We View Ourselves** Amitai Fraiman
37	**Proudly Jewish and American** Rabbi Rachel Ain
42	**Seriously, Honestly, and Joyously** Rabbi Jason Fruithandler
47	**To Be Seen** Rabbi Debra Newman Kamin
53	**Jewish Advocacy: Privilege and Permission** Rabbi Jack Moline
61	**When Amtisemitism Becomes Us – and What We Must Do About It** Rabbi David Evan Marcus
81	**Neither Silenced Nor Afraid** Jonathan Fass
87	**Privilege and Vulnerability after the Pittsburgh Shooting** Sarah Rudolph
94	**Shema** Julia Knobloch
95	**Olam Chesed Yibaneh: Building this World from Love** Rabbi Claudia Kreiman
113	*Contributors*

Introduction: Loud, Proud, & Jewish

This book is both a response and also a response to response. Let me explain what I mean with a personal story.

My daughter stood, proud and ready, as our rabbi stood to bless her upon becoming Bat Mitzvah. Joyous family and friends were present, and light, filtered through majestic stained-glass windows, filled the sanctuary. Suddenly an alarm sounded:

> *"This is not a drill. This is a lockdown. Please stay in place and await further instructions."*

It turned out to be a system malfunction. But in the 16 minutes between the alarm going off and our knowledge that it was a false alarm, it felt dreadfully real. The fact that this happened after weeks of violence against the Jewish communities of nearby Monsey and Brooklyn, NY, made our fear all the sharper.

Synagogue leaders remained calm, the police speedily responded, and with precision. An older women, who had just moments before handed out prayerbooks, was one of many who swiftly double-bolted the sanctuary doors and guided those around her.

My daughter's older sister was the one who, in the middle of others sending urgent texts to loved ones and quietly comforting each other, captured the idea that prompted this book's emergence. She looked at me, with tears in her eyes, and said,

> *"Abbah, I'm not afraid. I think we're going to be fine. But why do we live in a world where this happens?"*

She's right. She's one hundred percent right. We are fine. Our community's skill and preparedness avoided irrational alarmism and pollyannaish obliviousness, protecting not only our bodies but also our souls.

But for so many others, alarms aren't false. The growth of nationalism (especially White Nationalism in America), the mistrust being sown between segments of society, the alarming rate of antisemitism across the globe, the hate from the highest echelons of political power (and, more importantly, its acceptance with a shrug by vast swaths of society) – all of this means that the danger is real and that the alarm is not false.

And, because of this reality, it is all too easy to be on the constant alert, to feel headlines pounding in our consciousness, and to feel constantly threatened. The incessant "fight or flight" adrenaline in our blood is no way to live healthily. And as one contributor to this volume put it, the danger of the Jewish community remaining in a state of alert is most dangerous because it allows those "who hate us and seek our destruction to define us. We must not let them dictate how we view ourselves."

And so, prompted by one daughter's glorious Bat Mitzvah celebration and one daughter's clarion call for a better world, I invited the authors who have graced this collection with their visions to suggest ways for Jews to be unapologetically Jewish and not become insular. In other words, I asked them to help us all to find a formulation of Jewish Pride that stands in and for the world, not against it.

To quote the great historian and author, Howard Zinn,

> *"What we choose to emphasize in this complex history will determine our lives. If we see only the worst, it destroys our capacity to do something. If we remember those times and places – and there are so many – where people have behaved magnificently, this gives us the energy to act, and at least the possibility of sending this spinning top of a world in a different direction."*[1]

And, as the great historian Deborah Lipstadt recently put it,

> *"While we stand guard – we would be crazy not to – we do so in order to be free to celebrate Jewish life in all its manifestations."*[2]

May we be blessed to remain strong, safe and joyful, committed to amplifying the bright, purposeful light of the tradition we solemnly swear to protect.

> Menachem Creditor
> January 27, 2020
> Rosh Chodesh Shevat 5780

---

[1] You Can't Be Neutral on a Moving Train, (Beacon Press, 2002)
[2] "The Best Way To Fight Antisemitism? Jewish Joy" (The Jewish Forward, October 23, 2019)

Foreword

This is Our Moment
Melanie Roth Gorelick

This year, as we celebrate the 75th Liberation of Auschwitz, we are also confronting a rise in antisemitism, globally and locally. Much to our dismay, our efforts to make the world more tolerant and safer seem like they may be unraveling. It can feel, based in old trauma and centuries of Jewish history, as if we could soon be outcasts and welcome no more in our homes.

Over the past several decades, with antisemitism at its lowest in history, many Jewish organizations moved community resources from engaging in civic spaces and standing with other minority groups to priorities such as peoplehood and the Jewish future. We have learned from our work to counter the Boycott, Divestment, and Sanctions movement that leaving these spaces has created room for anti-Israel and other haters to influence. We also allowed mainstream civic engagement issues and human rights to be labeled issues of the "left" and those on the right try to make the case that social justice and *tikkun olam* are actually not real Jewish values.

Furthermore, some on the left do not see the need for a big tent. Is it possible for the Jewish community to come together to define both a definition and a strategy to stop antisemitism in its track?

Our response must be multi-pronged: relationship-building with other faith, racial and ethnic groups, creating narratives to make our case, seeking funding to secure our institutions and houses of worship, ensuring Holocaust education around the country, tracking and documenting hate crimes and organizations online and new laws and regulations, and advocating with our elected officials to do more such as creating taskforces on antisemitism, and more.

These grass-tops efforts are important but will they stop growing antisemitism and hate?

And let us remember to ask the questions essential to our greater society: Are we doing enough to build a just and pluralistic America? Are we standing with other communities on issues where they feel vulnerable, persecuted, and hated? Are we speaking out when a black person is profiled or killed by police in our communities? Are we standing up with our Latino and Muslim neighbors when executive orders and ICE raid their homes, separate them from their families, and create fear-messaging against them? Are we involved in civic life including how our local policies related to housing, education, and employment will help elevate the lives of those in poverty? Are we ourselves running for office, sitting on non-Jewish charities with our Jewish civic engagement hat on? Are we sharing with others our values of justice and fairness, so we know our neighbors and they know us? Are we ensuring that as we secure our own institutions, we are not harming others as part of unintended consequences?

This is our moment. We must calibrate for today's specific challenges. We must counter hate with love, fear with support, and again be active visionaries and participants in the country and world we want to live in partnership with those with whom we co-exist.

> *Melanie Roth Gorelick is the Senior Vice President of the Jewish Council for Public Affairs (JCPA).*

Raise up the Joy!
Rabbi Annie Tucker

In Poland, in the late 1930's, there lived a family by the name of Peltz. Mr. Peltz was a great builder and it was his custom to erect the family's sukkah[3] each year immediately after Yom Kippur, placing it in a prominent location where the entire neighborhood could admire its beauty and splendor.

The year the Peltz' son, Moshe, turned seventeen was a terrible one. News of the war had reached Poland and the Peltz family knew that the Nazis could not be far away, but this did not stop Mr. Peltz from building his beloved sukkah. The family decorated it with paper chains and hanging fruit, placed inside it a table laden with fine china and flowers, and gathered in the sukkah to begin the holiday together.

Just after they had finished making Kiddush, the Peltz' began to hear the sound of hobnailed boots. And before long, a large German officer leading a troop of angry

---

[3] A sukkah is a temporary shelter covered in natural materials, built near a synagogue or house and used especially for meals during the Jewish festival of Sukkot.

soldiers entered the sukkah. The holiday dishes were cruelly swept off the table and the Peltz family was led to the center of town where they were packed into trucks and sent away to concentration camps all over Europe. As a final salvo, the German officer and his soldiers systematically tore down the Peltz' sukkah.

Moshe Peltz now lives in Israel where he is married with two children. And every year at this time, he gathers with his family along with other survivors of the Holocaust in his sukkah where he recites the traditional words that we insert into Birkat HaMazon (the Grace after Meals) during the Sukkot holiday,

> *"Harahaman, hu yakim lanu Sukkat David hanofelet – May God raise the fallen sukkah of David."*

"I have lived to see the fulfillment of this prayer," says Peltz. "God has finally raised the fallen sukkah of my parents."

I feel like Jews have been dwelling in booths for the past year, if not longer. I am not speaking here of individuals who struggle under conditions of abject poverty and quite literally have nowhere permanent to sleep, but rather am thinking even of the rest of us - nestled comfortably in our houses and condos, sleeping on soft mattresses under warm blankets. We have been dwelling in sukkot because, as antisemitism continues to rise in this country and around the world, we might feel suddenly less comfortable outwardly proclaiming our Jewish identity than we've felt in a long while.

We have been dwelling in sukkot because in a post-Pittsburgh and post-Poway world, where as recently as this very Yom Kippur two Jews were murdered in Germany by a gunman attempting to enter a congregation in order to wreak havoc, we no longer feel fully safe and secure in our own sacred houses of worship. We have been dwelling in sukkot because even here in Westchester County recent months have brought Swastikas in a high-school bathroom in Scarsdale and the Kol Nidre desecration of our White Plains Holocaust Memorial. We have been living these past many months in a state of true fragility.

Celebrating Sukkot in Manhattan immediately after September 11th over eighteen years ago, I was struck for the first time by the odd paradox that this festival of vulnerability, of placing ourselves in flimsy, temporary structures exposed to the elements, is also referred to as *Z'man Simchateynu – the time of our great happiness.*

How strange it is that this season of fragility, of leaving the comfort and security of our homes to instead open ourselves up to the perils of the world around us, should be seen as a time of joy and celebration! For most of us, Sukkot's themes of uncertainty and exposure are associated with anxiety and worry rather than festivity and delight. How did this holiday, so focused on the precarious nature of human existence, come also to be one of exhilaration?

One of the traditional explanations for Sukkot as the Festival of Joy comes from its connection to the Israelites' period of desert wandering, for our time in the wilderness was one not only of incredible vulnerability but also one of intense connection to the Divine. During this period God traveled before us in a pillar of cloud by day and fire by night, provided us with manna to eat and water to drink, covered us with *Ananei haKavod – the Clouds of Glory*, and eventually ushered us into the Promised Land. Like young children, we were completely dependent upon God's Providence as we wandered through the desert, and as a result we enjoyed an extremely intimate relationship with the Divine, one different in many ways from the kind of relationship that we enjoy today.

The holiday of Sukkot represents a return to our desert existence – a time when we were incredibly needy and fragile, yet incredibly well cared for and protected, not unlike a new-born infant. By making ourselves vulnerable, we open ourselves to finding shelter, not from the strong roofs of our homes but instead from the strong hand of God in Whose Presence we dwell for the eight days of the festival. Returning to this early stage of intimacy brings us great joy!

While I find this traditional conception of Sukkot to be quite beautiful, I also acknowledge that it may feel difficult for many of us, living in a world of anxiety and fear, to feel sheltered by God's presence in this volatile climate. And so I think that there is perhaps another reason why the holiday of Sukkot is associated with joy – or at least with hopefulness – a reason that is illustrated by the poignant story of the Peltz family and their sukkah.

My teacher, Dr. Ismar Schorsch, former Chancellor of the Jewish Theological Seminary, teaches that for him the sukkah is a metaphor for the Jewish condition, for the great strength that our people have had to survive inhospitable climates and thrive despite overwhelming odds. The sukkah may look weak and fragile, may even be toppled easily by a heavy wind or a Nazi boot, but it is actually the very symbol of strength and resilience, representative of our peoples' ability to survive impossible conditions and even now –thousands of years after the first sukkot were built – to continue to follow the proud tradition of our ancestors.

If the rabbis indicate that Sukkot's joy comes from feeling close to God, Dr. Schorsch indicates that the holiday's elevated spirit comes from recognizing our own well springs of strength and resilience, our ability to overcome adversity and survive when times are very difficult indeed. Whether it is the rise and fall of a Polish sukkah or the rise and fall of antisemitism in our country, there is great comfort in recognizing that we come from a long tradition of survivors. We have the inner resources to withstand the inevitable ups and downs of human experience.

Walking around White Plains these last few days I have been struck by a strange, beautiful juxtaposition. First, I have seen sukkot of every shape and size start to pop up in backyards and on driveways, atop porches and decks. It is an incredible marker of the kind of Jewish community in which we live in to see how many individuals and families build sukkot for the holiday here, and it is a strong statement of identity – even in this period of uncertainty and caution – to so publicly mark our homes as proudly Jewish ones where we will practice our traditions without fear.

Alongside these colorful sukkot, I have also seen the Halloween decorations of our neighbors start to appear – bright pumpkins and delicate spider-webs, spooky ghosts and bony skeletons. Halloween, too, is in many ways a holiday about fragility; it ushers in the "dark" period of the year and represents the precarious liminality between existence and mortality as it was seen as the night on the calendar when the barrier between the living and the dead was thinnest. At this time when all of us feel at our most exposed, we create an environment where our disparate traditions live side by side in harmony. We conquer fear with expressions of peaceful coexistence.

At a recent community vigil in White Plains, I was struck by the size of the crowd pulled together last minute and in the middle of a busy work day. I was even more struck by its diversity – individuals of different ethnicities and faiths all standing side by side. An antisemitic act of vandalism was perpetrated by but one individual, but the response from our community was loud, strong, and united: love is stronger than hate.

It strikes me as unfortunate that it often takes the worst of times to bring people together for right; perhaps some of the answer to combatting the terrible intolerance sweeping through our country is to create more opportunities to come together even on good days, so that we may come to know the "other" making it that much harder to dehumanize him. Maybe this, too, is some of the reasons for Sukkot's paradoxical joy. Vulnerability often leads us to build bridges in a way that we don't necessarily do during periods of greater strength.

And, as I wished my community during the most recent celebration of Sukkot, trading the steady comfort of our homes for the unique pleasure of dwelling in booths that are exposed, flimsy, impermanent. May we reach for the joy of feeling God's protection during this fragile time, for the strength and resilience that these modest huts represent, for the hope of seeing our own holiday trimmings standing side-by-side those of our neighbors.

May this truly become *Z'man Simchateynu – a time to rejoice*, despite those things that make our world so scary. May God continue to raise the fallen sukkot of David, here and everywhere.

My Mom Used To Say...[4]
Ruth Zakarin

My mom has been gone for over four years now, and to this day, there are about a thousand things that trigger my memories of her: the smell of chicken soup on my stove, the first notes of a Carole King song coming up on my playlist, the feel of her ring on my finger. My mom was quite the news hound, and I still have the impulse to pick up the phone to call her every time there is a major political development, which has been nearly every day these past two years. After this year's midterm elections, I imagined how delighted she would have been with the new generation of women staking their place in the halls of Congress, how proud she would be of her grandson live-tweeting election results. This is to say, her absence remains very present for me.

Lately, I have found myself thinking a lot about something my mom used to say to me when I was growing up. Let me first admit that, as for so many kids, a great deal of my

---

[4] This essay was originally published on the Jewish Women's Archive and appears here with the permission of the author.

mom's "important stuff to tell me" went in one ear and out the other. But one of her sayings lodged itself in my brain, not because I found it to be particularly wise or insightful, but because it drove me nuts every time she said it. It was her go-to statement whenever she was cajoling me into doing something she considered a mitzvah, especially when I wasn't exactly jumping at the opportunity. She would look at me with that, you know, mom look, and say, "Do good things and tell people you're Jewish."

I would look right back at her and... roll my eyes. I found this to be such an old-world, almost paranoid way of thinking. Like we should prove that Jews are good people by being extra nice and then saying "Hey, did I happen to mention that I'm Jewish?" I grew up around Holocaust survivors, so I understood the lingering worry about how the rest of the world viewed Jews. And like so many others in the Jewish community, I bought into the collective pride when someone famous turned out to be one of the tribe — did you know that Paul Newman has a Jewish parent? But overall, my mom's saying never sat well with me.

Shouldn't you do good things just for the sake of doing good, and not as an advertisement for the Jewish people? Yes, history had not been kind to us, but this wasn't Germany in the 1930s, it was heavily Jewish Long Island in the 1980s. I was lucky to live in a community where I didn't have to think about being Jewish and what that meant to my existence in the larger world. I became involved in social justice causes from an early age, but felt absolutely no need to put myself out there as a Jew when I engaged in this work.

That feeling has carried well into my adult life. I have dedicated my career to addressing and ending domestic and sexual violence, and wherever I've worked, folks have known I was Jewish. There's nothing like taking endless days off in September/October to highlight one's Jewishness. But until recently, I never really brought my Jewish self to my work. I never expressed that my commitment to social justice is grounded in my identity as a Jew.

What changed this? A few years ago, I became involved with an interfaith coalition in the city of Brockton, Massachusetts, where I have worked for several years. The executive director of the coalition asked me to speak at a May Day rally for immigrant rights, and she wanted me to touch on the intersection between immigration policies and safety for survivors of domestic and sexual violence.

I spent a great deal of time thinking about what I would say, and how I could communicate my personal investment in and connection to these issues. I was particularly sensitive to the fact that I was a white woman speaking about an issue that overwhelmingly impacts people of color, and talked through this concern with one of my coworkers who was also going to speak at the rally. During this conversation, I shared with her some stories from my own family history, stories that had led me to care so deeply about my chosen work.

My grandfather told me many stories about his upbringing, including the experience of growing up with a very violent father. I shared some of this with my coworker: How he and his five siblings would take turns staying with Ida Zakarin, their mother, in her room at night to protect her from their father, who would often return from his late night shift at work drunk and enraged. How Ida, my great grandmother, spoke no English and was dependent on her American-born children for everything from translation assistance to protection from her husband's violence. How my great grandparents came to the United States fleeing the pogroms of Russia, leaving behind family and livelihood for an uncertain future. I explained that I came to this work because I couldn't imagine what it was like to be Ida Zakarin, living in fear in a country that was not her own, without the ability to communicate with others outside her family. I didn't want anyone else to feel that way, ever.

Sharing this story aloud reminded me that I had always brought my Jewish self to my work because my Jewish story inspired me to do this work in the first place. And the Jewish liturgy and teachings about welcoming the stranger continue to fuel my passion for this work. At the rally, I recognized the power of sharing this part of myself with others; my Jewish immigrant story allows me to connect with other folks and their stories. It is my sincere hope that it has also allowed them to feel a deeper sense of connection with me. I have since made it a point to bring lessons from my faith and family history to my work towards culture change and social justice. It just feels more authentic to do so.

Given that, I would like to propose a small amendment to my mom's saying. Instead of "Do good things and tell people you are Jewish," I'd prefer to say this: "Do good things with and for others, and bring your Jewish self when you do so." Do the hard work with folks who are nothing like you, but be clear about who you are and the history that informs you.

I'd like to think that my mom would approve.

How We View Ourselves
Amitai Fraiman

There are many things I love about being Jewish. So, when antisemitism rears its ugly head, I like to remind myself of a few of them, because beyond the physical harm antisemitism causes, there is another price we pay as a community: the damage to our collective consciousness and sense of identity. When we are not under attack, we have the privilege – and obligation - to delve into the positive aspects of our identity, to explore questions of meaning and purpose, and to give expression to our deepest values. But when we are threatened, we get pushed into an "us vs. them" mentality. We are brought together by fear and hate – and have no time to deal with lofty ideas. We are thrown down the Maslovian pyramid and forced to focus on our most basic human need - security.

That is yet another detrimental result of antisemitism. Having been exposed to antisemitism from a young age, I am well aware that it is hard to compare physical and spiritual harm. However, our sages assert that the tyrants who sought to crush our spirit and way of life were worse than those who sought to destroy our bodies. The reason is that while the body is finite, the soul is infinite, and hence the harm is indelible. Indeed, the damage to our spirit can last for generations, while physical suffering, as horrific as it may be, is ephemeral.

In this vein, I believe it is crucial that in dark times like the present we must focus with even greater determination on our spirit, our morality, and our identity. We must ensure that those who hate us and seek our destruction do not define us. We must not let them dictate how we view ourselves. It is in this vein that we must reaffirm our pride in our Jewishness - and our refusal to cower and disengage from the world.

So what do I like about being Jewish? What makes me proud? Everything. From the most mundane to the most profound. From bagels and humor to Jewish memory and meaning-making. From *kibbitzing* to *kabbalah*. *Tzedaka*. *Purim*. *Tzitzit*. Tradition and innovation.

Yet there is a fundamental element which makes me especially proud of my Jewishness– and which I believe is in the

DNA of our identity, at the very inner core of our being. It is the tension in which we are called upon to live our lives. It's the tension between the idea that the world was created for us and the notion that we are nothing but dust and ashes. It's the tension between the demand that we preserve our tradition intact, and the idea, expressed within that very tradition, that there are moments that we must go against our tradition to preserve it. It's the tension between *chesed* and *din*, *lovingkindness and judgment*, and the list goes on.

The common thread is that we are destined to live in constant discomfort, in a never-ending balancing act - never static, never standing still. Indeed, the idea of struggling is embedded in our name - *Yisrael*.[5] Our very name is a call to action: a call to struggle both with God and with our human reality - not to accept things as they are, but to follow an unending path towards improvement, both personal and collective. Being Jewish means being restless. It means not accepting fate, but instead taking control of our destiny. It means adopting a countercultural outlook. The Kuzari tells us that the very foundation of our belief is rooted in heresy. Indeed,

[5] Genesis 32:29

Abraham's smashing his father's idols[6] was an act of defiance - and we are collectively expected to live accordingly.

The same energy fueling our lives in a constant search for balancing opposing ideas is that which fueled Abraham: the constant questioning of the status quo. And that is why I love being Jewish and why I'm proud of it.

Beyond posing a physical and spiritual threat, our current reality highlights a specific tension for our community, namely, that between the particular and the universal. It is a tension reflected in our holidays, rituals, and prayers, one that demands we find a balance between focusing on the unique aspects of our identity, and being open to the outside world. It is hard to achieve that equilibrium, especially in moments when we feel under attack and our instinct is to retreat inward.

We must resist that reflex lest we endanger the very fabric of our identity. First, it upsets the delicate balance between the universal and particular. Second, it runs counter to the very demand to struggle: disengagement is

---

[6] See the commentary of Rashi on Genesis 11:28.

the easy way out. Lastly, retreat is a reflexive response to external forces - not an expression of agency and choice. I'm proud of my Jewishness. It is unwavering, and I will not let the forces of darkness dictate to me how I interact with the world, and how my Jewishness is manifest in it.

Am Yisrael Chai!

Proudly Jewish and American
Rabbi Rachel Ain

If you were with me at the Mets game during Passover, you would think the entire stadium was Jewish. You wouldn't imagine that we are only 2% of the world's population, and given the ability to have kosher food, including a "K for P"[7] bun, you certainly wouldn't think that there are people in this world who don't want us around...In fact, as Tal Kienan writes in his book, God is in the Crowd,

> *"America represents a zenith in Jewish history, at which Jews have achieved numerical concentration unprecedented in the Diaspora, financial prosperity, and political power. They enjoy the option of overt, unapologetic Jewish identification that, in their neighbor's eyes, does not negate their Americanism."*

Or so we thought.

Sitting at the ballgame last week, proudly a NYer (don't tell my DC family I said that)

---

[7] "Kosher for Passover," a special label affixed to foods prepared in accord with the rituals of Passover.

and proudly Jewish, I was thinking about a line in our Torah:

> *You shall not copy the practices of the land of Egypt where you dwelt, or of the land of Canaan to which I am taking you; nor shall you follow their laws. My rules alone shall you observe, and faithfully follow My laws: I the Lord am your God.*[8]

REALLY? Isn't this exactly what I was doing – finding a way to "have it all?" To sit at a game w/my baseball hat on, eating a K for P hotdog, and counting the *Omer*?[9]

So what does this actually mean to not copy the practices of the land? Are we really to remain truly separate?

We are in fact, NOT supposed to remain completely separate. We are supposed to stop at stop signs. We are supposed to pay our taxes. We are supposed to get vaccinated. This is known as *"Dina D'Malchuta Dina - the law of the land, is the law."*[10]

---

[8] Leviticus 18:3
[9] The seven weeks of counting the Omer spans the 49 days between the second day of Passover and the beginning of Shavuot.
[10] Babylonian Talmud, Tractate Nedarim 28a

But we must ask: is there a difference between law and culture? For example-can we continue to follow the law and be proudly Jewish? Of course we can! What does it mean when we choose to take a standardized test on a Sunday and not a Saturday? How do we live, simultaneously, in both worlds? And do we lose anything when doing so?

Two medieval interpreters read the verse in a more restricted light. Rashi understands this as applying only to the Egyptians and the Canaanites, who were "more corrupt than all other nations." Abraham ibn Ezra (12th century Spain) explains that this stricture applies to the Egyptian legal system.

Both of these sages perceive that there is much to be learned from the wisdom of non-Jews. Not only in the realm of science, but also in human relations, Jewish traditions have been open to insights from other peoples. The key, both to this Torah verse and to the later interpretations, lies in the final biblical phrase.

Those non-Jewish practices and insights which strengthen Jewish survival, which sensitize us as a people, which teach us how to be more loving, more caring and more sensitive, which prompt us to understand more about Judaism and to practice it more fully, pose no threat to our Jewishness.

On the contrary, we benefit from their inclusion. An openness to learn, however, should not be mistaken for the blind adoption of all non-Jewish standards.

So maybe what we are being taught to do is not become like the other but bring our culture to the larger one in which we live.

So where does that leave us? How do we engage with who is around us and remain proudly Jewish?

First, we need to look at current events and know that unfortunately, no matter how at home we feel, we always need to remember who we are…we need to be aware that there has been, sadly, an uptick in antisemitism, and yet again, just last week saw how hate has infiltrated our communities. Maybe it is our destiny to be a tiny bit apart….

Towards the end of God is in the Crowd, Kienan postulates that there are four core values that exemplify what it means to be

Jewish: Community, Tradition, Challenge, Dissent.

I believe that if we can hold on to these, even when living amongst others, we don't need to disappear. We don't need to hide. We don't need to be afraid. We can be proudly and unapologetically Jewish and celebrate all that that means.

Seriously, Honestly and Joyously
Rabbi Jason Fruithandler

I hear this phrase and I imagine a parade of Jews wearing big foam fingers in the shape of Jewish stars, of kippot (skull caps) that light up and flash colors, or perhaps dancers with long beards balancing bottles on the top of their heads. These kind of surface expressions of pride are beautiful, fun and cathartic.

But. if I choose to dive deeper though what makes me loud and proud to be Jewish is tricky to answer. On the one hand, it might feel dangerous to be proud to be Jewish because it might hint that Jew-*ish* is better than some other kind of "*ish*." On the other hand, it is daunting to be Jewish because as an "insider" I know so many things Jewish people, culture and tradition have gotten wrong! I feel anxious to even approach the topic.

Is there an articulation of Jewishness that, without hesitation, invites the specialness and greatness of other ways of being? Is there an articulation of Jewishness that does not attempt to cover up our flaws and failings? In other words, is there a space in which I am unequivocally loud, proud and Jewish?

I am most proud of my Jewishness when it expresses itself seriously, honestly and joyously.

In order to explain serious Judaism I have to make a confession: *I kiss the Torah*. When it comes around on Shabbat morning, I touch it with my hand and kiss it, and when I have the honor of putting it back in the ark I kiss the Torah directly before I close the doors. My university education tells me this is absurd! I was trained to be a skeptic: to tear down every argument, to find the base human need that propels a leader's actions, or to breakdown any ritual, rule or norm to its least meaningful, basest components. I can tell you that kissing the Torah is illogical, mildly idolatrous, and clearly about inculcating a sense of subservience to the larger group.

And yet, despite my skeptic-training, I choose a serious approach to Judaism. It means closing my eyes when I say the *Shema* (an essential Jewish prayer) and letting that matter. It means taking ancient pride in my *Magen David* (Jewish star) even though I know it is a late medieval invention. It means seeing the Shabbat candles that are not clearly mentioned in the Torah as holy.

Taking Judaism seriously means believing there is real meaning to be found in its traditions and history.

Honest Judaism, though, means acknowledging that there is not always meaning to be found. It means confronting the darker parts of our past and owning our own failings. Those moments I allow to be meaningful are *earned* by facing the truths of our imperfect tradition. We do have a history of buying into the patriarchy that has so plagued Western civilization; we do have a story of different leaders creating rules that maintain their own power (eg, some approaches to Kashrut developed into a system to keep Jews separate from non-Jews). We are only at the beginning of figuring out how to be truly inclusive with LGBTQ people. There are so many other examples.

Owning these truths allows me to look at other groups and say, "My group is not better than yours, and yet we have something to offer." Honesty helps me hold my head high, change what must be changed, and find meaning anew in what will be retained.

Finally, I am proud of my Judaism when it is fun. Or course, Judaism must sometimes be heavy, but at its core it is a tradition of joy. When the Torah tells us that we must "*Chai baHem – live by these rules and regulations,*" I believe firmly that it means we must celebrate them. We must learn to laugh, cry, cheer and groan together.

It is the ultimate balance to the true danger of any tradition that hopes to understand the One Creator of All. I can too easily take myself too seriously. And so, while I find meaning in *tefillin*,[11] I must also laugh at just how silly we must look! I wish to approach Torah study with a smile on my face, to enjoy delicious Shabbat dinner and to find humor in this strange, paradoxical and surprising world of ours.

I am loud, proud and Jewish when I watch two Jews under the chuppah laughing through each other's imperfections as they declare their love for each other to the world. I am loud, proud and Jewish when I read

---

[11] Tefillin, worn on the arm and head during weekday services, is a set of black leather boxes containing scrolls of parchment inscribed with verses from the Torah.

about the Israeli volunteers who are the first responders to natural disasters all over the world. I am loud, proud and Jewish when I join a group of Jews who have no good reason to believe God exists and yet pause their High Holy Day conversation because it's time to sing *Avinu Malkeinu* (a Jewish prayer with a beautiful tune that asks God for help) with one voice.

In this current climate of division, hatred, and fear, my Jewish pride has nothing to do with those who hate us. I am loud, proud and Jewish when I am being serious, honest and laughing with joy.

To Be Seen
Rabbi Debra Newman Kamin
Excerpted from High Holidays Sermon 2017

How many of you have ever played the game "peek-a-boo I see you?" Do you know that is actually a universal game that many cultures play with their children? From a young age we have the very human need to be seen.

If there is anything I can say about our country in these last two years or so, is that we have competing visions of who feels seen and who does not. Identity politics at its best (and I think identity politics is almost always at its worst) shows a deep yearning for each group to feel that their narrative is seen, heard and validated. I have learned over the past year that, as a Jew, I am not exempt from that need.

In this past year where we have suffered through so many incidences of antisemitism, I kept thinking about the end of the movie *Schindler's List*. At the end of the movie the Jews turn to one of the soldiers and ask, "where should we go"? He answers "Don't go east; they hate you there. Don't go west;

they hate you there." If I look to the right, I see the victims of Pittsburgh and Poway and the burning torches and hateful chants of Charlottesville and if I look to the left, I see BDS and anti-Zionism pretending not to be antisemitism. I see Jewish students on campus made to feel guilty, marginalized and shamed if they care about Israel.

But we are also marginalized when antisemitism occurs from White Supremacists. There was something that I noticed in the aftermath of Charlottesville that I found extremely upsetting. In the immediate days after Charlottesville I heard loud voices from both the left and the right unequivocally stating that they explicitly condemn racism and hatred and bigotry, as they should, as we all should. But I wanted them to say something else, I needed them to say that they condemn antisemitism. It was only when Frontline aired the footage of men marching with torches shouting "*the Jews will not replace us*" that people began to call out antisemitism as well.

But I am not just worried about physical violence. I am also worried about the effect that antisemitism has *on our souls*. I think it has a profound effect on our psyche, both when it comes from the right *and* when it comes from the left.

When it comes from the right, we are tempted to repeat the very old trope,

> *"In every generation there are those who rise up against us."*

Everybody hates us, they have always hated us, and because we have already lost and everybody already hates us, we become single-issue voters. We vote for politicians only based on where they stand on Israel and not how they stand on many other issues that we need to care about. It also sometimes leads us to justify, without pause, Israel's actions. During the Gaza War I heard people say we should flatten Gaza; they already hate us. So, when antisemitism comes from the right, we are tempted to excuse any bad behavior on the part of Israel because everybody hates us.

But I am, in truth, more worried about antisemitism that comes from the left. Our college campuses today have become a place where political correctness dictates that Jewish students can only see themselves as beneficiaries and embodiments of white privilege. Israel on the campus is often demonized. The left-wing McCarthyism that is practiced on campus today shames Jewish young people who support Israel and shames them into silence about their own identities. I worry that it is causing a new form of self-hatred.

We are the only minority in America who gets attacked both from the right and the left. And sometimes left-wing antisemitism and right-wing antisemitism actually meet and share common cause. Roger Waters, a member of Pink Floyd is vociferous when it comes to Israel, BDS – boycott, divestment and sanctions – and really sees it as his personal mission to harass any artist that is scheduled to perform in Israel. On David Duke's website, there is a page in praise of Roger Waters.

I preferred the days when the phrase was "minorities" since we are included in that category. When we switched to "people of color" Jews were excluded and lumped with the White majority.

One of the things that we have learned from the LGBTQ community is that we no longer assume just by looking at someone that they are a man or a woman. We need to ask "what is your pronoun?" They will tell you and then you will give them the respect of calling them what they want to be called even if you thought their appearance led you to believe something else.

In our daily prayers, the *Shema* tells us "not to follow after your eyes."[12] Seeing is not believing and your eyes can actually lead you astray. We should not assume anything about anybody until we ask them. As a Jew I would like that courtesy extended to me as well.

Just because I appear to be white, I have a specific religious and cultural experience that makes me different. I have my own experience and all that I ask is for you to give me the respect of wanting to know who I am.

And I know my community has a lot of economic privilege, but no one needs to preach that to me. I have a 3,000-year-old tradition that tells me what to do with my privilege, "feed the hungry, clothe the naked, care for the needy and always strive for justice."[13]

---

[12] Numbers 15:39
[13] Isaiah 58

There is a beautiful poem in *Siddur Lev Shalem*[14] written by Merle Feld:

> *We want so much to be in that place*
> *Where we are respected and cherished,*
> *Protected, acknowledged, nurtured,*
> *encouraged, heard*
> *And seen, seen*
> *In all our loveliness,*
> *In all our fragile strength*
> *And safe, safe in all our trembling*
> *vulnerability. Where we are known*
> *And safe, safe and known*
> *Is it possible?*

---

[14] Published by the Rabbinical Assembly (2016)

Jewish Advocacy: Privilege and Permission
Rabbi Jack Moline

Some thirty years ago, the brand-new JCC in my community was defaced with swastikas and misspelled graffiti. Even then, Northern Virginia had more of a DC vibe than what we "immigrants" believed was the latent bigotry in the other parts of the Commonwealth. We were outraged, but we were not afraid. Within forty-eight hours we had gathered there – men, women and children – to hear our community leaders and clergy exhort us to stand up to such prejudice.

I was there with my two young daughters and my in-laws. And when, in the middle of a long-winded speech by our member of Congress, the JCC received a bomb threat, I was handed the megaphone to continue the rally in the parking lot as responders swept the building. My family was close by. When the gathering ended, we loaded up the car and headed home.

We were five minutes into the drive when my five-year-old burst into tears. She blurted out, *"Why would anybody want to hurt us?"*

My mother-in-law comforted her in the back seat. I was piloting a ton of steel on a busy highway at 55 mph and could do nothing immediate about the sudden surge of homicidal rage I felt toward the person or persons who stole my child's innocence.

The teenagers responsible for the vandalism and threats were arrested. They are now deep into their forties. Their parents are senior citizens. Do I have any reason to believe that what motivated them to this hate crime, this act of domestic terrorism, this child abuse emerged in a moment and disappeared with a fine and probation? Of course not.

So, what is different about 2020 that we are shocked, shocked at acts of Jew-hatred and believe there is a resurgence of anti-Jewish sentiment here in the United States and around the world?

The answer, I believe, is a combination of privilege and permission.

The place in society my parents believed they earned is now presumed as normative by the American Jews who are their children and grandchildren. We worked hard for more than a hundred years to transition from immigrants to self-sustainers to integrated members of the general society. The aid societies founded to rescue our European refugees now advocate for general immigration reform. The hospitals we built to employ our doctors who could not get hired elsewhere are now part of health care conglomerates. The defense agencies we developed to combat antisemitism are now staffed by allied non-Jews who have an equal focus on discrimination in general.

I believe that those are all good things.

However, they have led us to assume that the rest of America has followed our trajectory. And it is not true. While we have been living increasingly as white people of privilege, the progress toward affluence and opportunity has not been matched by poorer people of every color and ethnicity, and certainly not by the portion of the African American community with whom we have minimal contact.

Our aspiration to achieve the American dream has been realized in the most identifiable strata of society: politics, media, finance, academia, professional careers. The increased visibility has made us convenient targets of the individuals on both the right and the left who have inherited or discovered a proclivity to scapegoat the Jews.

The JCC did not cause the vandals to deface it. However, their disdain for Jews likely would have remained private without a target. The growth of the Jewish community shook loose the poison fruit.

Fifty-some years ago, a Nazi named Frank Collin led a small band of Jew- and Black-haters in my hometown of Chicago. He had a daily recorded message that spun fantastic tales about the depravity of both groups and invited comments on voice mail. It was a regular activity for my friends and me to call the number and leave derogatory messages. It felt like a game, even when Collin and his Nazis sought to march through the town of Skokie, home to many Holocaust survivors.

Collin ran for alderman in Chicago in the 1970s and garnered 16% of the vote in his ward. People of voting age then are at least grandparents now, having raised or influenced two new generations of voters. (I can presume that a similar percentage of Jew-haters on the left have continued their own legacy.)

Collin was repudiated far and wide. Those who supported him – 16% of his neighbors – were mostly considered extremists and crackpots. Few if any of the remaining 84% voters said to their children, then or now, "I hope you grow up to be like Frank."

I do not believe that the percentage of people on the right or the left politically who hate Jews is larger than it was in 1975. (And please remember – it was not 16% of the general population. It was 16% of his mostly-white ward.)

I believe that tolerance for the expression of Jew-hatred has increased. Bigots now believe they have permission to exercise their First Amendment rights with impunity, and, frankly, they do. The legal right has always existed in America. The cultural norm has shifted. I could point to any number of trends that have converged to make such hate speech attractive to the purveyors, but merely uncomfortable for the general population. It is no longer disqualifying to citizenship to protect hate speech toward Jews or anyone else.

You may be waiting for me to point a finger at your favorite political villain. I won't. No individual or group of individuals has caused this drift in society. They are symptoms, not causes. Today, Frank Collin would not have an answering machine hooked up to a landline to spread his message of hate. His audience would not consist of the few who knew enough to listen and respond. His message is no more compelling in the mouth of an extremist activist – just amplified and more easily accessed.

I do not have the academic or journalistic chops to challenge those who have chronicled the apparent rise in anti-Jewish sentiment in the United Sates and around the world. I will say only that it just does not feel right. More non-Jews love Jews enough to marry them in a month than hate Jews enough to beat them in ten years. That former cohort has demonstrably increased. Despite the horrifying and high-profile crimes against my people in these most recent times, they remain isolated and mostly anecdotal. The perpetrators on both sides are inspired to pre-existing conditions, not surrendering to contagion.

So, what are we to do, if that is the question of the hour?

First and foremost, we must understand our privilege. Inculcated by our tradition as we are by the historical precariousness of Jewish life, we tend to hyperbole and hysteria to build a fence around our survival. I don't argue against it – I felt it on behalf of my little daughter – but I commend engaging with others who deserve such privilege as well but have not yet achieved it. In the end, like justice, until everyone has achieved the American Dream, nobody has. Privilege is not a limited commodity, despite the name.

I have tried to act on this advice through a lifetime of activism on behalf of the values I understand as the essence of Jewish tradition. Most especially, I have been purposeful about reaching across the boundaries of faith, race and ethnicity while bringing my genuine Jewish self. The older I have become, the more I have understood that being an ally means mostly being a follower. I constantly struggle against my impulse to tell other communities what I think they need to do. In contrast, I try to use my voice to address the noxious qualities of bigotry that remain too deeply rooted in segments of our Jewish community.

Frank Collin is not the only one with a 16% following.

At the same time, our advocacy as Jews must be as much about permission as about rights or privilege. My teachers before me made clear that being a faithful Jew means taking responsibility in the world, not demanding opportunity. We must model in small ways and large that, however difficult it may be, responding to bigotry with bigotry, stereotype with stereotype, incivility with incivility is a recipe for increasing, not decreasing permission for bad behavior. Speaking truth is not about trying to out-offend. It is about calling to community and inspiring an accounting of the soul.

I plead against hysteria and hyperbole. I plead for principle and progress.

Oh – and I demand you get out and vote.

When Antisemitism Becomes Us - And What We Must Do About It
Rabbi David Evan Marcus

The courthouse where I preside stands barely a mile from Orthodox communities in Rockland County, New York, that have been withstanding one vicious antisemitic attack after another. After an especially bloody incident shook the local Jewish community and made national headlines, one person after another came into my judicial office – shaken, inwardly wrestling – asking me, as a pulpit rabbi, whether God would want them to buy guns for self-protection.

"*They*," I hear repeated over and over again, "are out to get *us*. *They* always are out to get *us*." Sure enough, public reports confirmed that gun permit applications in the area soon surged along with urgent calls for anti-terrorism courses and synagogue security upgrades.[15]

---

[15] Brum & Esposito, "Monsey Attacks Prompt A Call to Arms as Weapon Training, Self-Defense Courses Surge," *The Journal News* (Jan. 5, 2020); "Monsey; Levine, "Gun Applications Surge in Rockland County after Hanukkah Stabbings," *N.Y. Post* (Jan. 14, 2020).

As *Rolling Stone* magazine reported, whole communities previously on record to loathe armaments and so-called "target-hardening" suddenly aligned on gun policy with the National Rifle Association. Said one prominent defender of Hasidic community's run on guns:

> *"Jews, just like everyone else, have the right to bear arms.... The panic and violence have been created by hate crimes [and] current assaults ... not innocent people looking to defend themselves."*[16]

That same week, I taught about antisemitism at a schoolwide forum at the Academy for Jewish Religion, the pluralist seminary I serve as faculty in rabbinics and theology. I described a recent service mission I co-led to Jewish Cuba, where I was moved to learn from Cuban Jews that they have no personal experience of antisemitism. Both publicly in Holocaust memorial displays and privately behind closed doors, communities of Jews across Cuba insisted that the antisemitism latent elsewhere – that in the United States and Europe periodically erupts into hate and

---

[16] Dickson, "After Hanukkah Stabbing, Some Ultra-Orthodox Jews Are Arming Themselves," *Rolling Stone* (Jan. 3, 2020).

violence – simply does not exist in modern Cuban experience:

> *Es que en Cuba ni siquiera saben lo que significa el antisemitismo. Un cubano no lo sabe. Usted le dice que algo es antisemita, y le preguntará, "¿Qué cosa es eso?"*
>
> *In Cuba, one doesn't even know what antisemitism is. A Cuban simply doesn't know. You say to someone that something is antisemitic, and the response is, "What's that?"*[17]

Dozens of ostensibly open-minded seminary students shook their heads in disbelief and even disdain. Instinctively, they couldn't seem to wrap their heads and hearts around the idea that, in the 21st century, there might exist Jews living publicly and proudly as Jews without antisemitism – even despite substantial evidence to that effect. For my North American and mostly Caucasian seminary students, Jews and antisemitism so inexorably inter-are that this putative "fact" is beyond any reasonable doubt. Like their Rockland County co-religionists but generally more liberal in outlook, a number of my students – all of them future rabbis and cantors, leaders of 21st century Jewish life entrusted to nourish Jewish bodies,

---
[17] La Sinagoga Centro Hebreo Safardí, La Habana, Cuba (2019).

hearts, minds and souls – came up to me insisting, with varying degrees of discomfort, that some unidentified *they* always are out to get *us* and that *we* would be misguided or worse to pretend otherwise.

The instinct that antisemitism inheres in Jewish experience says as much about the condition of the Jewish spirit as about the societies in which Jews live. That this instinct simultaneously pervades both ostensibly right-leaning Orthodox communities and ostensibly left-leaning pluralist and liberal Jewish communities, at the same time, should rivet our attention at this moment when antisemitic and anti-Jewish hate are spilling over yet again. This observation is not to diminish the virulence of hate or mitigate the necessity of speedy, sure and salient response. Rather, this observation is to expand what we mean by "salient response" to include wise and careful spiritual focus on the Jewish psyche itself.

Catch-22 author Joseph Heller presciently observed that "Just because you're paranoid doesn't mean that they're not out to get you."[18] The seemingly ever-present and cyclical realities of anti-Jewish hate – from

---

[18] Heller, *Catch-22*. New York: Simon and Schuster (1961).

century to century (then) and social media click to click (now) – cannot but singe the Jewish soul. If we are deeply honest, we must acknowledge the truth of this impact alongside the important practicalities of battling antisemitism by every wise physical and political means at our collective disposal.

After countless generations of Jews have been targeted for calamitous prejudice, hatred and violence, Jews should forgive ourselves if some of us believe that some *they* always are out to get *us*. *Fiddler on the Roof* made dark humor of it. The Passover Haggadah prominently proclaims it: "In each and every generation, there are those who stand against us to destroy us.[19] And not without reason: prominent antisemitism scholar Dr. Deborah Lipstadt rightly describes antisemitism as humanity's most pervasive and pernicious hatred – *the* hate of all hates – that seemingly will not be extinguished because it is so utterly beyond reason and so often aroused purposefully for nefarious social and political purposes.[20] The Passover Haggadah, while a ritual and

---

[19] Haggadah, Maggid, *V'hi sheamdah*.
[20] Lipstadt, *Antisemitism: Here and Now*. New York: Schocken Books (2019).

educational masterpiece of its time, thus also speaks a timeless truth of history: most every Jewish generation does indeed seem to experience anti-Jewish prejudice, hatred and violence somewhere. Tragically, my seminary students and Rockland County colleagues were correct to that extent.

But *somewhere* and *often* do not mean *everywhere* and *always*. Put another way, description is not prescription: what has been is not necessarily inherent – even if it exists now.

The individual and collective traumas that arise in response to both historical and present-day antisemitism naturally impel the trauma-impacted psyche to be vigilantly on guard. As psychologists and sociologists know all too well, the natural response to both individual and collective traumas is to rehearse, retrace and relive those traumas. These dynamics have both neurobiological reasons (traumas re-pattern neurons to fire and wire together, cutting deep "wagon tracks" in the mind) and psychospiritual reasons (we naturally seek to make meaning of our lives, so we rehearse experience to create coherent narratives of explanation and identity).

Partly for these reasons, over time Jewish souls and communities that so often have needed to navigate hate also have come to expect hate and even react internally to hate before hate occurs. Said Dr. Ziv Cohen, a prominent psychological scholar and clinician who described his practice now full of Jews – many sent by their rabbis – struggling to navigate the modern realities of the antisemitism:

> *"Trying to use denial [as a psychological defense mechanism] would make you seem quite divorced from what's going on. I think what you're seeing is a lot of folks shifting from denial to hyper-vigilance, a state of alarm, a state of fear, a state of anxiety."*[21]

Fueled by these natural dynamics, clear-headed preparedness too often morphs into a well documented pattern of spiritual exhaustion, on the one hand, and hyper-arousal, on the other. In turn, these can reshape Jewish identity in relationship with itself and the world. As Rabbi Dr. Tirzah Firestone and others long recognized, such is the collective inter-generational "Jewish PTSD" that often gets triggered when

---

[21] Kramer, "Anti-Semitic Attacks Breeds Anxiety: 'It's their worst nightmare coming true,'" *The Journal News* (Jan. 21, 2020).

antisemitism rears its ugly head.[22] This triggering fuels the inner instincts of hyper vigilance, alarm, fear and anxiety – creating a feedback loop that can accelerate on itself.

This intergenerational trauma – arising from historical antisemitism and Jewish response to it, absorbing the proliferation of traumas past and present even to the point of inwardly fusing with the anticipation that these traumas will repeat – is one reason that so many of my seminary students couldn't imagine any Jewish life not currently experiencing virulent antisemitism. It's the same kind of reason that otherwise thoughtful people can sound so angular in declaring, as if an article of faith, that *they* are out to get *us*.

These dynamics ask us to understand them deeply, with sensitivity and compassion. Understanding these dynamics, however, does not mean – must not mean – that we should accept them as unalterable givens of Jewish life. Such acceptance would connote a passivity and even fatalism that render us Jews as psychological and spiritual victims of these inner dynamics, even as we stand up powerfully against hate. Inner victimhood-

---

[22] Firestone, *Wounds into Wisdom: Healing Intergenerational Jewish Trauma*. Rhinebeck, N.Y.: Monkfish Publ. (2019).

type dynamics in response to antisemitism, Lipstadt writes, are the fount of both inner exhaustion and inner hyper-vigilance – and both are deeply problematic for Jewish life. That is why we must focus on what antisemitism does to the Jewish soul, and take spiritual steps as bold as the practical steps that anti-Jewish hate demands.

This spiritual focus means acknowledging some difficult truths, even at risk of triggering inner recoil against them. One pernicious effect of antisemitism is that some Jews minimize their Judaism: we try to "pass" so as not to attract attention or align with dynamics of suffering and subjugation. Another is to jolt Jewish minds and hearts into an instinct that anti-Jewish hatred is so inherent that we learn to expect and see antisemitism where it does not exist. Beset by a seemingly constant drumbeat against Jewish existence much less Jewish thriving from some corners, and tolerance or weak protest by the broader societies in which Jews live, we may come to believe that withstanding antisemitism (often alone, *us* against *them*) is part of what it means to be Jewish. We might even take on this kind of resistance-based identity as an emblem of Jewish pride.

Either way, whether or not we intend to do so, we stitch antisemitism into the fabric of who we are – not in the derogatory "self-hating Jew" kind of way, but by accepting the expectation that Jews will and even must suffer for being Jews. In turn, we and Jewish life often respond with self-protective counter-xenophobia – fueled by alarm, fear and anxiety – that ultimately are inconsistent with spiritual health and Jewish spiritual values.

Put simply, even as we combat antisemitism outwardly with all we've got and in every sphere of action, we also must combat antisemitism inwardly. That's why antisemites – utterly repugnant as their paranoid beliefs and destructive behaviors are to Jews and to all civil society – do not top Lipstadt's worries about antisemitism. "As much as I worry about what the antisemites might do to Jews," Lipstadt wrote in October 2019, "I worry even more about what we might do to ourselves because of antisemitism."[23]

We are hardly the first generation to grapple with these ostensibly "softer" spiritual facets

---

[23] Lipstadt, "The Best Way to Fight Antisemitism? Jewish Joy." *The Forward* (Oct. 23, 2019).

of response to antisemitism, which tend to get lost in the urgency and noise of antisemitism's tumultuous waves of hatred, violence and recrimination. The rabbi of the Warsaw Ghetto, Kalonymus Kalman Shapira of Piaseczno ("The Piacesner Rebbe"), wrote in 1940 that the desperately lethal conditions of Nazi occupation and eventual extermination of Jews – which we might imagine to justify a spiritual focus only on survival and immediately necessary responses – instead compelled the *most* spiritually internal approach. The greater the external threat, Shapira wrote, the greater the urgency and duty to focus inward on the Jewish soul – lest it become beleaguered and experience itself as separated from the inner softness and vulnerability of sacred experience.[24]

Through the lens of Rabbi Shapira's words in the Warsaw Ghetto, and antisemitism scholar Lipstadt's admonitions now, I look anew at my received tradition and see antisemitism's scars on the Jewish soul and Judaism's tapestry of sacred text and spiritual practice. At Passover seders that

---

[24] Shapira, *Aish Kodesh* on P. Shemot 5702 (January 10, 1942). Nanuet, N.Y.: Feldheim Publ. (2007), at 217; Miller (Worch trans.), *Sacred Fire: Torah from the Years of Fury*. Northvale, N.J.: Aronson Press (2000), at 260-261.

tradition deems a religious and cultural mandate for all Jews of every generation for all time, we proclaim the ever-presence of antisemitic destruction as an article of identity and faith.[25] In conversion rituals that rabbinic tradition sets as Judaism's front door, the Talmudic conversion script informs would-be Jews – at the very initiation of the conversion ritual – that they are poised to join a hated people:

> "Don't you know that the Jewish people at the present time are anguished, suppressed and harassed, and hardships are visited on them?"[26]

A whole tractate of Talmud, *Avodah Zara*, takes as a central focus and factual given the strained relationship between Jews and "others" arising from the latter's victimization of the former.

Against that seemingly constant onslaught, Talmud's rabbis responded that Jews will prevail "in the end" and that the "nations" – in Talmudic terms, mainly the Romans, Persians and early Christians – someday will quake before God for their mistreatment of

---

[25] Passover Haggadah, *supra* n.5.

[26] B.T. Yevamot 47a. The rabbis even responded that a would-be convert who explicitly acknowledges this truth and nevertheless wishes to join the Jewish people is "immediately" accepted. *Id.*

the Jews.[27] Hard baked into their response was a xenophobic ban on many kinds of neighborly engagements with the "nations," ostensibly so as not to encourage their religious ways but probably as much to self-protect against encountering others, their words and their actions. As if in response, core Jewish liturgy of the Amidah even "prayerfully" invokes: "To the slanderers [among the nations], let there be no hope: let all [their] wickedness perish in an instant, and all Your people's enemies swiftly be cut down."[28]

Just as I look at these historical textual imprints of Jewish experience with antisemitism, I look to the self-protective invective that circulates in modern Jewish life. As a child attending a Jewish day school in New York, I remember the school's dubious choice each year to herd young students into a darkened gymnasium on *Yom HaShoah*, Holocaust Remembrance Day, to sit in small circles on the ground while pictures of Nazi death camps flashed on the walls. In reply to concerns that my parents tried to raise about the content and context

---

[27] B.T. Avodah Zara 2a-3a.

[28] Amidah, *ad loc. Lamalshinim*. This traditional blessing has undergone numerous changes over the centuries, shifting in focus from intra-Jewish sectarianism to relations between Jews and surrounding dominant powers.

for young children, school administrators sharply labeled my parents "self-hating Jews" and "antisemitic" – either unaware or uncaring that my father was raised in Israel and both of my parents were active in Jewish life.

In the decades since, including years as pulpit clergy, I have winced to hear how often some of my co-religionists instinctively and angrily respond that something or someone is "antisemitic," without pause for self-reflection or reasoned inquiry as to other possible legitimate, non-prejudicial explanations for whatever might rankle them. While deeply thoughtful people can disagree legitimately about whether a certain comment or policy might reflect anti-Jewish invective, the regularity and speed with which otherwise thoughtful Jews can snap that something is "antisemitic" is jarring, worrisome and deeply sad. Time and again, I hear from deeply caring Jews much the same kind of refrain I keep hearing from courthouse co-religionists and seminary students: with pain in their voices, they say – and sometimes shout in defiance – that some antisemitic *them* is out to get *us*, or that the *they* of majoritarian life won't care.

It's time for a high-priority Jewish spiritual response to complement all our necessary hands-on outward responses of allyship, security, protest, legislation and prosecution. It's time for a high-priority spiritual response because we should not be content with a bunker-mentality Judaism, one that becomes safe in body but prickly in heart. The future of a Judaism of love, compassion, softness, inclusion and resilience hangs in the balance.

So what to do? While the contours of a full response are beyond the scope of any short article, I have some suggestions. One is to make an individual and collective commitment that the spiritual and tangible go hand-in hand. It's why my synagogue created a "Task Force on Antisemitism *and Spiritual Response*" – understanding that education, advocacy, security and deep introspection must come together if they are to be fully authentic, sustainable and effective.

A second is to name and explore the inner Jewish dynamics in the wake of antisemitism as a core commitment of synagogue and Jewish community life. It will take care, time, courage, and well-trained professional assistance to facilitate in community contexts the rough-edged thoughts and feelings that may get aroused. It may be unpleasant; some people may not engage; and we can imagine all kinds of political reasons why synagogue leaders might resist this kind of programming as a central offering. But ultimately there is no wise alternative unless we are content – as individuals and as a people – to let these kinds of inner dynamics fester in the Jewish soul. There is no wise alternative unless synagogues and other Jewish community institutions are content to abdicate true leadership on this vital issue that touches the heart of every Jew.

A third is to arouse and harness the healing properties of empathy in outward focus. While the Holocaust is unique in global history for many reasons – no fair comparison exists between the scope, political dynamics and global impact of the *Shoah* and any other experience in human history – it takes nothing from the singularity of the *Shoah* also to allow that Jews are not the first or only people to experience genocide or bear the inner scars of inter-generational trauma. If we are wise – and *Pirkei Avot*[29] teaches that the wise can

---

[29] Pirkei Avot is a compilation of the ethical teachings and maxims from Rabbinical Jewish tradition.

learn from everyone[30] – then we can ask what lessons we might draw from others who experienced collective suffering, even if their suffering is not what Lipstadt called antisemitism's "hate of all hates."

For instance, my synagogue began with a facilitated political, cultural and psychological exploration of the second generation after the Rwandan genocide, in which over 800,000 were murdered in just 100 days (then speedily more than double that number). Not surprisingly, the North Americans who are most involved in second-generation Rwandan recovery are Jews.[31] By asking and caring about others who have suffered – and specifically learning how Rwandan self-concept, psyche and spirituality shifted in the wake of genocide – we Jews can arouse our compassion and apply those lessons inwardly.

A fourth is to make antisemitism and spiritual response mandatory academic and spiritual concerns at every Jewish seminary and every clergy association continuing education system. If 21st century Jewish

---

[30] Pirkei Avot 4:1.
[31] Deep thanks to Edward Ballen of the Rwanda Education Assistance Project for his exemplary leadership, commitment and compassion.

clergy are to fulfill their roles to care for Jewish bodies, hearts, minds and souls, by definition clergy must become adept at navigating not only the external landscapes of antisemitism and community response but also those internal landscapes. By extension, 21st century Jewish clergy must navigate their *own* internal landscapes and their own experience with and response to antisemitism; what they mean for their journeys in spiritual service; and the impacts on how they walk their theology, trust and faith in the world. I am grateful that the Academy for Jewish Religion has begun taking this important step for its seminary students.[32]

Recently I was moved to read from Rabbi Shapira in the Warsaw Ghetto a beautiful *midrash*, drawing from Zohar, that sheds light on the spiritual journey we must take in the wake of antisemitism and intergenerational trauma. When God prepared to create the world, God and Torah (existing supernally, long before Sinai) debated whether to create humanity. Torah told God that because humanity is sure to sin and bear culpability, humanity also is sure to

---

[32] Deep thanks to Dr. Ora Horn Prouser, Rabbi Dr. Jill Hammer, and Hazzan Michael Kasper for visioning this important initiative.

fear its own destruction by divine judgment. "Is it for nothing," God responded to Torah – with the words that Torah later would recount God speaking to Moses in the cleft of Sinai rock, words that would become core Jewish liturgy – "that I am called 'God of mercy, gracious, long of patience'?"[33] Shapira deduced that it wasn't God who created fear: it was Torah that created fear by speaking it and assuming it.[34]

Many a spiritual adept has taught about how we can harness fear (in Hebrew *yir'ah*, also "awe") for wise spiritual development. As Lipstadt aptly observed, we can harness the fear of what antisemitism does to the Jewish soul to arouse our self-awareness, compassion and inner vigilance against despair and counter-xenophobia.

At the same time, inspired by our forebears' resilience and learning some lessons they didn't yet learn, we can chart Jewish lives keenly aware of physical and political realities, and also shining with spiritual audacity – insisting that instinctive fear, reclusion, otherness and othering are not

---

[33] Zohar II:69b, Exodus 34:6.
[34] Shapira, supra n.10.

inherent in Jewish life and ultimately are unacceptable in Jewish life, no matter what.

As both Lipstadt and Shapira put it, ultimately the best way to fight antisemitism is the opposite of fear – a maximalist and expansive Jewish joy.[35]

---

[35] Lipstadt, supra n.9; Shapira, supra n.10.

Neither Silenced Nor Afraid
Jonathan Fass

As I opened my e-mail on Thursday, November 8, 2018 my heart sank. Pouring into my inbox were a chain of e-mail messages and on-line news stories about a series of swastikas that had been drawn on sidewalks across Stamford, CT.

As a Stamford resident and Jewish professional, in a bedroom community of New York City with approximately 10,000 Jews, I was heartbroken that hatred had shown its ugliness in my friendly and left-leaning town. This was not the first antisemitic act in Stamford and I knew it would not be last, because each morning I read about the growing hatred against minorities that was fueling America's right-wing voices to unprecedented levels. The Unite the Right rally of August 2017 is where "Jews will not replace us" became a clarion call to anti-Semites across America. Nearly a year later, and only twelve days before the swastikas appeared, was the massacre at Tree of Life synagogue in Pittsburgh. I was scared for myself, my family, and for the community I served.

To make matters worse, November 8 was the evening of our agency's Seventh Annual Schoke JFS – Saul Cohen lecture, which brought together over 200 community members for a widely promoted, free, and open to the public lecture by a Jewish leader. The lecture was held downtown at the public library, and the largest of the swastikas found was drawn just outside the library's main entrance, with the words "Good Luck" below it. I had walked past the library just the afternoon before, in my final preparations for the lecture the following evening. A second swastika had been placed just outside a location we were purchasing as new offices. Although nothing indicated an explicit link to our agency, the coincidence of events could not be avoided.

Our agency sprang into action to consider our options and obligations to the community. Members of the Board of Directors, the lecture committee, and leaders of other Jewish organizations began to contact us. The leadership expressed concerns about ensuring the safety our audience, our staff, and our speaker. However, we also needed to consider the concerns of the library, our caterer, and library patrons not attending the lecture.

While some voices, perhaps for their own sense of comfort, minimized the threat, others suggested we cancel the lecture immediately. Of primary importance to me was understanding how law enforcement could assist us in our decision-making process. So, my first call was the Stamford Police Department. I was relieved to hear that the police were aware of our lecture and were already considering additional safety precautions.

The police recommended establishing secure access to the library, a visible and significant police presence around the building, and a bomb-sweep prior to the lecture. I was assured there would also be "invisible" precautionary measures taken. Unless you are familiar, these conversations tend to elevate anxiety. Nevertheless, our agency felt that law enforcement was able to provide a safe space for our lecture to proceed as planned. This message was shared with our leadership, our speaker, our colleagues at the library, and staff. Every person who was a stakeholder in the event needed to feel comfortable with moving forward. The next question to address was how to share this message with the community.

In coordination with the police, our Federation sent an email to the Jewish community, encouraging us to make every effort to attend the lecture, as a sign of solidarity and message to the perpetrator that fear would not keep us away.

As we prepared for the lecture later that evening, we continued to be in contact with law enforcement and library staff. When I arrived later in the afternoon to review the space, it troubled me how incidents such as this force both the Jewish community and our larger community to pull resources from other challenges.

Why should Schoke JFS, dedicated to helping the most vulnerable of Stamford, now need to develop a significant security budget?

Moving into our new offices just a few months later, our agency allocated thousands of dollars for security that might have otherwise been used in fulfilling its core mission. As I walked past the bomb sniffing dogs that evening, I silently prayed for quiet.

Close to three hundred people attended the lecture that evening. Our lecture committee acknowledged the larger than normal crowd and thanked them for their courage. Beyond that, the lecture went ahead as usual. Everyone agreed that giving more attention to earlier events detracted from our purpose for gathering and gave the perpetrator even a small victory.

When the guests had gone home and the caterer was cleaning up, a member of the library staff approached me. He shared his disappointment in how the current climate of hate has grown. "I'm sorry," he said, "that your community has to go through this every once in a while." I shared my frustration as well, but also my appreciation to the library for allowing the evening to continue. "Canceling was never an option," he replied, "because we are a community institution, and the Jewish community is part of that community."

Driving home, I thought about the famous picture of Rabbi Abraham Joshua Heschel marching arm-in-arm with Dr. Martin Luther King Jr. and others at a 1965 march in Selma, Alabama. I've often wondered if Heschel was fearful that day. Perhaps, but it didn't stop him from showing up, despite the obvious danger in doing so. The first march had ended in bloodshed just two weeks earlier. While I can't bring myself to liken our community's actions to that of the Civil Rights Movement, I do feel a connection to Heschel's courage and moral outrage. Three hundred strong we marched ourselves into the library and the larger Stamford community supported us. Like Heschel, our feet told our story. We would not be silenced. We would not be afraid.

Privilege and Vulnerability after the Pittsburgh Shooting[36]
Sarah Rudolph

The day after the shooting in Pittsburgh, I walked into Starbucks, intent on settling down with my laptop to get some work done despite the overwhelming distraction of mourning 11 of my fellow Jews who were just murdered in their synagogue two hours away from where I live.

I looked around at my fellow patrons, determined not to view them with suspicion, but unable to keep from wondering. I wondered whether they noticed me, whether they realized I'm Jewish like those tragic victims in Pittsburgh yesterday. Usually unaware of the scarf on my own head, that day I felt marked, standing out like a sore thumb. "Sore" is an understatement for how I felt that day, and I wondered whether the people around me knew, just by looking at me, how I might have been affected by a mass murder that might not look like it had anything to do with me. I wondered where their sympathies

---

[36] This essay was first published on thewisdomdaily.com/after-the-pittsburgh-shooting-i-feel-like-a-target/ (11/12/1018) and appears here with the author's permission.

lay, whether they saw me as I am, or whether, like Mr. Bowers, they saw me as some sort of a threat.

At the height of the police shootings that led to the Black Lives Matter movement, I felt conspicuous as a privileged white person and kept looking for ways to show the black people I encountered that I was on their side, that I saw them simply as humans and was horrified at the loss of innocent lives. Lacking the confidence to actually say anything to anyone, I satisfied myself with making a point of smiling and nodding at any person of color I passed; walking into a Starbucks, I would make a point of holding the door open for any black customers coming in at the same time. I knew it wasn't much, and even felt a little silly, but I hoped it was worth something.

After Pittsburgh, I didn't feel as much like a privileged white person. For the first time in my privileged little life, I felt conspicuous in my own status as a minority. I looked around me in Starbucks that day hoping for those random smiles and nods that would tell me I have friends.

I refuse to view my fellow humans with unfounded suspicion, but raised on

Holocaust history and the cry "Never again!" my mind can't help idly wondering – if it came down to it, would that guy over there shoot me or would he hide me? What about that woman; if my children were cowering in terror and she heard an errant cry, would she turn us in?

I don't even have Holocaust survivors in my family, to have trained me to think that way; I'm so firmly American that several of my great-grandparents were born here. But this is how we begin to think, when we begin to feel the threat of those who have irrationally decided that Jews in America pose some sort of a threat.

Funny; I don't feel like a threat. But I'm starting to feel threatened.

I cherish the email a non-Jewish friend sent when she heard about Pittsburgh. "We're grieving with you. How are you doing?" I tell myself she would hide my family, if America ever came to that.

I tell myself to stop thinking like that, and myself asks me how I can possibly stop.

A week later, I'm getting on a plane. I used to fly frequently, but it's been a while, and

I'm newly aware of the need for all that security. I bag up my liquids without complaint, smile and thank the TSA agent, grit my teeth and pose for the machine I despise but that will, I hope, catch anyone who might be a true threat and reassure us those of us who make it through that we don't need to fear each other.

I make a point of smiling and nodding at anyone whose eye I can catch – no longer to show them I don't think they're a threat, but in the hope they won't see me as one. As if all the smiles in the world could counter irrational prejudice and hatred, once it's taken root.

A woman asks me to watch her bag while she goes to the bathroom. Twenty years ago, when I flew all the time, I would have agreed without question. But too much has happened since then, and I hesitate. "You're probably better off taking it with you," I say. Not wanting her to think I actually suspect her of anything, I shift the blame to protocol. "If anyone comes and asks… Probably better if you take it."

Do I really think she's a danger, that her bag contains some sort of weapon she managed to get past security?

Does she, perhaps, now view me with suspicion because I wouldn't do her that one kindness? Did she walk away thinking, "Oh, those Jews, unwilling to help someone who's not their kind!"

It's a risk I have to take, because I have to consider the risks if I don't. But it frightens me.

I settle into my seat on the plane and pull out my crocheting. I checked before packing, to make sure my little crochet hook was allowed on the plane. It's not much of a weapon, but sharp enough that I warn my kids away from it, and I can't help wondering whether it will make the people around me nervous. Will they wonder whether my needlework is just a cover for some nefarious plot involving that little piece of metal? I start crocheting furiously, to show my intentions are innocent; I really do just want to crochet with it.

I can't help wondering, too, whether it's sharp enough to use for self-defense.

Do my fellow passengers see me as a threat, because of the scarf on my head or simply the Jewish blood in my veins? Should I consider them as potential threats, keep my crochet hook at the ready, because maybe someone among them agrees, inexplicably, with Mr. Bowers?

This is how we start to think.

And what is it that I'm crocheting? Yarmulkes for a bar mitzvah; matching Jewish head coverings for twin boys who will soon celebrate their growth into Jewish men. And I wonder, as I work, whether they are like me at their age, beginning to learn the horrifying elements of their history, but secure in the knowledge that they're safe here in America – or whether they are afraid like our ancestors, wondering who their real friends are. Afraid like I am now.

I felt silly when I made a point of smiling at black people in Starbucks just because they were black, but now I look for those smiles from others. I look for every burst of friendliness that tells me my scarf and my blood don't matter, that there are people – most people, enough people to overcome the others – who see Jews like me simply as humans, people who are as horrified as we are at the loss of innocent lives.

And I decide my crochet hook really is a weapon, but not that kind. It's a weapon I pray will prove mightier than any sword, any firearm, any bewildering propaganda that makes my people out to be something we're not. It's the weapon with which I will continue to create those symbols of Jewish pride.

As I crochet, I'm fighting for my right, and the rights of all, to walk the streets with scarves, yarmulkes, any covering or no covering. Our rights to live and smile and embrace each other regardless of whose blood flows through our veins. Our rights to live in this country with pride in who we are, and to never have to hide.

Shema
Julia Knobloch

Say it when the priests go eat the sacrifice.
Say it when the stars appear.
Say it until midnight.
Say it before dawn.
Say it in the morning light.
Say it when you rise, when you lie down,
in the desert, in walled cities,
in your house and on the road.

Teach it to your children.
Teach it to your children,
that they may say it,
say it when they wake,
when no stars are in the sky,
when time has no season
say it when the trains pull in,
say it at the ramp,
say it in the barracks.

Listen
to the words of the Shema,
put one ear onto the tracks
and listen,
you can hear it
through the grass, in the forests, by the river.
Listen,
learn it
teach it
say it
with all your heart, and soul, and might.

Olam Chesed Yibaneh: Building this World from Love
Rabbi Claudia Kreiman
Yom Kippur, Kol Nidre 5780

Close to 20 years ago, I lived and worked in downtown Jerusalem. This was the time of the second intifada, the violent Palestinian uprising of years 2000-2001. It was a time of frequent terrorist attacks by suicide bombers, attacks carried out in busy streets, in cafes and on buses. Over time, together with everyone else, I learned the routine we all followed after an explosion: Check in with your loved ones, let them know you are ok, ask if they are ok, check on anyone you know that could have been in that area or on that bus and then move on, do the next thing you were planning to do, as if nothing had happened.

At the time, some people called that being accustomed to reality, some people called it resilience, and some called it numbness. I, too, tried to respond this way. I really wanted to be able to move on with my life as if nothing had happened. I didn't want my experiences of trauma to get in the way of the very full and wonderful life I was living in

Jerusalem. But I was not always capable of responding so stoically.

One day, a suicide bomber blew himself up in a crowd very close to my downtown office. Close enough for me to hear the explosion, the sirens and everything that followed. I was supposed to go to a meeting of my fellowship of rabbinical students, but I had to wait until the streets were cleared again for people and traffic. This particular meeting was of a very close group of friends and teachers who met monthly to study Torah and to discuss our spiritual and rabbinic journeys.

My first reaction was to assume that the meeting would be cancelled. I called my mentor, Rabbi David Lazar, but he asked me - why we would cancel the class? In tears I responded, because there was a bombing.

He said to me, "because of the bombing it is even more important that we gather to study!"

I got very angry at him and explained, through my tears, that in my experience after a bombing the world stops -- you cannot simply go on as usual. But my teacher would not relent. He insisted I come to the class, and that he would not allow me to be immobilized by mourning and fear.

So, reluctantly, I went.

However, at the meeting we did not study what was originally planned. When we sat down to learn, I was so upset that my colleagues did not respond with the same intense sadness and fear that I was feeling, that I challenged them on this, angrily. They listened to me and they embraced me, they held me while I cried. They asked me to reflect on my life, to look at the strength I had found within me in the past, and to notice that I had not let fear define me. They embraced me with love, and together we moved on to study Torah.

Last October, when we heard the news of the shooting in the Tree of Life synagogue in Pittsburgh, we of the North-American Jewish community knew that something had changed for us. Eleven people were killed while in shul at shabbat services.

This was the deadliest antisemitic incident in the US. Unfortunately this was not to be a unique incident and it happens in the context of many more acts of antisemitism, including the shooting in the synagogue in Poway, California last April and many incidents of vandalism on Jewishly identified property, the most recent being the shattering of a Brooklyn synagogue's windows during our most recent Rosh Hashanah.

We also know that this is not happening in a vacuum. These are hardly the first examples of this kind of violence, and Jews are hardly the only targets. This is part of a terrible spate of violent hate crimes over recent years by white supremacists, in houses of worship, in clubs and in many other places.

There are too many to name by now, but I will recall two: the murder of nine African Americans by a white supremacist at a Charleston church in 2015 and the mass shooting at Pulse, a gay nightclub, in 2016, in which 49 people were killed.

Sadly, this kind of violence is not new, but now it has directly impacted Jewish sacred space, and Jewish communities engaged in prayer.

Now that the pain of this violence has been brought close to home we must ask - How are we responding? How do we work to root out hate and terror so that it does not fester in the hearts of the people of our country? How do we maintain the feeling of safety within our communities?

The Shabbat after the Tree of Life shooting, the organized Jewish community responded by showing up. The American Jewish Committee called for a Show Up Shabbat, and millions of people of all faiths rallied around AJC's #ShowUpForShabbat initiative, packing synagogues in what became the largest-ever expression of solidarity with the American Jewish community.

Our Sanctuary was filled, like it is tonight at for *Kol Nidre* and we prayed and sang and cried together. Most importantly we committed ourselves to moving forward without letting fear define us, but instead putting love and Torah at the center as our guide.

That is easier said than done. We can sing *Olam Chesed Yibaneh / We Will Build This World from Love*, again and again but the fear is real and it expresses itself differently for different people.

In conversations with many of you, I hear people's fears: fear of coming to shul, fear of this new reality, fear of what it means to be Jewish in this time and place.

Fear not just as Jews, but as citizens of this world, and specifically of this country.

The world feels very scary.

We have spent many hours in meetings, talking about balancing our security measures with our core values of being welcoming, inclusive and open to all.

These conversations are manifestations of the large question that must be addressed - how do we move forward in this new reality? How do we not let fear define us and how do we summon love, *Chesed*, how do we summon hope to be our guide?

This sort of capacity is often addressed in the field of psychology. Some of you might know about the psychotherapy Internal Family Systems Model or as it is sometimes called Parts Work.

Here is an oversimplified introduction to the principles of this theory:

1) It is the nature of the mind to be subdivided into subpersonalities or parts.
2) Each part intends to contribute something positive to the individual.
3) No part is inherently or intentionally bad.
4) The goal of therapy is not to eliminate the negative parts, but to help those parts act in less extreme ways and to not take over the entire person.[37]

Personally, this approach has been very helpful to me. As my therapist says, the goal is to learn to speak for the part rather than from the part and not let my emotions, my anger, my sadness, my fear, my anxiety, those parts that can easily bring me down,

---

[37] With thanks to Rabbi David Lerner for summarizing this so eloquently. https://blogs.timesofisrael.com/how-our-parts-make-us-whole/

define me or take over my identity. Rather I am called to respond with compassion to those parts of myself, to love and listen to them so I can be my better self.

In their book *"Leadership on the Line, Staying Alive through the Dangers of Leading"*, Ronald Heifetz and Marty Linsky introduce the notion of "Sacred Heart."

In their analysis of leadership they speak about how cynicism, arrogance and callousness can mistakenly and dangerously define leaders. They write the following, which I think could speak to all of us at different times of our lives, both individually and as a group:

> *"The most difficult work of leadership involves learning to experience distress without numbing yourself. The virtue of a sacred heart lies in the courage to maintain your innocence and wonder, your doubt and curiosity, and your compassion and love, even through your darkest, most difficult moments… In one moment you may experience total despair, but in the next, compassion and forgiveness. You may even experience such vicissitudes in the same*

> *moment and hold those inconsistent feelings in tension with one another."[38]*

Rabbi Sharon Cohen-Anisfeld, my dear teacher and friend, told me she learned from our friend Rabbi Sue Fendrick to use the image of driving a car and to ask who the driver is, which are the emotions and values that drive us through life. When fear, anxiety and despair appear in our lives, we can acknowledge their presence, and even our inability to make them "go away", but we can also ask them to sit in the back seat, rather than drive the car. Can we do that as a community? Can we recognize the feelings of anguish, hopelessness and despair, that the current realities of our world and our country might evoke, and together, can we all move them to the back seat and invite Chesed, love, compassion, and loving-kindness to be the driver?

We find in the Talmud this rather challenging teaching:

---

[38] "Leadership on the Line: Staying alive through the dangers", Ronald Heifetz & Marty Linsky, pages 227, 228.

> *Rava, and some say Rav Ḥisda, said: If a person sees that suffering has befallen them, they should examine their actions.*[39]

This text is generally understood as claiming that suffering comes about as punishment for one's transgressions.

"Examine their actions" means to examine your actions so that you understand why whatever happened, happened.

For many years, I have read this text differently. I suggest that instead of reading it in the past tense- asking us to check what we had done wrong to bring about this suffering, we should read it in the future tense.

For me, *"examine their actions"* means that I must check my actions now - what do I need to change from now on?

How does this experience shape my future decisions about how I live my life? How do my own experiences of life, of suffering, of fear or loss, my experience of hurt actually help me shape my priorities from this point

---

[39] Babylonian Talmud, Tractate Brachot 5a

onwards, how do they shape my values and my journey?

These are the questions I invite you to ask.

These are the underlying questions when I say that we are in search for a response to living in times where antisemitic acts are growing, in times when hatred, injustice and hopelessness seem to be surrounding us.

How do we not let fear or anger or anxiety or skepticism, define us and how do we summon love and *Chesed*? How do we summon hope to be our guidance?

The Italian Jewish Holocaust Survivor Primo Levi, writes a heart-wrenching account of his experiences in Auschwitz in his book "Survival in Auschwitz". Auschwitz was abandoned by the German SS guards on January 18, 1945 which was ten days before Soviet troops arrived to rescue the prisoners. Primo Levi, who was a prisoner at the Monowitz labor camp in the Auschwitz complex. gives a detailed description of what happened during those ten days that the prisoners were on their own, without the Germans to keep order and feed them.

In one scene, Levi describes a moment in which three men, including him, repair a window and a stove, which were vital for their survival as they were about to freeze to death. He writes:

> *"When the broken window was repaired and the stove began again to spread its heat, something seemed to relax everyone, and at that moment Towarowsky proposed to the others that each of them offer a slice of bread to us three who had been working. And so it was agreed. Only a day before, a similar event would have been inconceivable. The Law of the Lager [the camp] said: 'eat your own bread, and if you can, that of your neighbor', and left no room for gratitude. It really meant that the Lager was dead. It was the first human gesture that occurred among us. I believe that, that moment can be dated as the beginning of the change by which we who had not died slowly changed from Haftlinge [prisoners] to men again."*[40]

Primo Levi identifies the moment of liberation, of the transition from prisoners to free people again, as the moment when they are able to share bread. Humanity is possible

---

[40] Survival of Auschwitz, Primo Levi, page 160

again, when people are guided by human generosity.

What made them human, what made them free, was their rediscovered capacity to respond with *Chesed*, with love and generosity to the most terrible reality that humans can possibly experience. They were able to summon love, to summon *Chesed* and that brought about the transformation of their lives.

The Israeli novelist Aharon Appelfeld in his essay on the 50thanniversary of the liberation of Auschwitz, published in the New York Times in January 2005, speaks of his experience as a secular Israeli and Holocaust survivor. In speaking of his experience, he quotes the words of a doctor from a religious background, who survived the Holocaust and who sailed to Israel with him in June 1946. Appelfeld writes:

> *"[He, the doctor] told us: We didn't see God when we expected him, so we have no choice but to do what he was supposed to do: we will protect the weak, we will love, we will*

> *comfort. From now on, the responsibility is all ours."*[41]

These powerful words must be heard in dialogue with the Talmudic teaching:

> *"... one should follow the attributes of the Holy Blessed One, Blessed be He... Just as God clothes the naked, ...so too, should you clothe the naked. Just as the Holy Blessed One visits the sick,... so too, should you visit the sick. Just as the Holy Blessed One consoles mourners, ... so too, should you console mourners. Just as the Holy Blessed One buried the dead, ... so too, should you bury the dead.*[42]

The Talmud text teaches us that the way we walk in God's path is by clothing the naked, visiting the sick, comforting the mourner and burying the dead. This doctor, whom Appelfeld quotes, experiencing God's absence, ends up responding in exactly the way our tradition teaches to be in relationship with God: by caring for others, by offering love to the world, by building a world with love.

---

[41] https://www.nytimes.com/2005/01/27/opinion/always-darkness-visible.html
[42] Babylonian Talmud, Tractate Sotah 14a

For many of us, fear, anxiety, disappointment and desperation are familiar feelings these days. A member of the community recently wrote on Facebook about the experience of coming to *shul*, to a new reality for American Jews -- a shul with a guard -- and the struggle to stay positive. I myself have experienced these feelings as I read the news, as I try to understand how it is possible that so much injustice, hatred, and racism are at the forefront of our reality in this country.

Fear is constantly being weaponized by leaders who want us to respond and act in the world based on our fears.

It serves them well, but it definitely does not serve us well, it does not serve our humanity.

Fear cannot be the driver of our life -- instead, we need to lead with *Chesed*, love, generosity, compassion, resilience and hope. We must continue to ask ourselves, again and again, how not to let fear define us and how to summon love, how to summon Chesed, how to summon hope to be our guiding beacon.

I will finish this on a personal note.

My mother was 48 years old when she was killed in an antisemitic terrorist attack in Argentina, the deadliest such attack outside of Israel since the holocaust.

My older sister Marianella, who celebrated her 48th birthday last April made a commitment that from now on, she will live for two. Have fun for two, volunteer and give love to the world for two. She has decided to live for our mother the part of her life that was cut short. My sister decided that instead of letting her pain, our deep pain, be what drives her in life, she would let her love for our mother be the thing that drives her.

May she be an inspiration for all of us to be driven by our joy, by the knowledge that we will not give up, that we do not freeze up, by the conviction that we can move forward with *Chesed* and love.

Olam Chesed Yibaneh.
We will build the world with love.

> *I will build this world from love*
> *And you must build this world from love*
> *And if we build this world from love*
> *Then God will build this world from love.*[43]

A world of love and not hatred.

A world of compassion not anger.

A world that is not defined by fear and helplessness but defined by resilience and hope.

A world in which we embrace each other and the world itself with love.

---

[43] Melody and English lyrics by Rabbi Menachem Creditor.

Contributors

Rabbi Rachel Ain is the Rabbi at Sutton Place Synagogue in Midtown Manhattan. She is actively involved in the community-serving as a co-chair AJC's rabbinic roundtable, the board of directors of UJA federation of NY, and the executive committee of the New York Board of Rabbis. She is in the clergy leadership program for the Institute for Jewish Spirituality.

Rabbi Menachem Creditor serves as the Pearl and Ira Meyer Scholar in Residence at UJA-Federation New York and was the founder of Rabbis Against Gun Violence. A frequent speaker in communities and campuses around the United States and Israel with over 1 million views of his online videos, he was named by Newsweek as one of the fifty most influential rabbis in America. His 20 books and 6 albums of original music include the global Jewish anthem *Olam Chesed Yibaneh* and the Rabbis Against Gun Violence anthology *None Shall Make Them Afraid*. He has been involved in the leadership of American Jewish World Service, AIPAC and the One America Movement, an organization dedicated to bringing together Americans of different faiths and opinions.

Jonathan Fass is the Chief Operating Officer of Elayne and James Schoke Jewish Family Service of Stamford, CT. He also directs the Behrend Institute for Leadership and the Kuriansky Teen Tzedakah Corps of the United Jewish Federation of Greater Stamford, New Canaan, and Darien.

Amitai Fraiman. Israeli/American. Husband. Abba. Rabbi. MPA. MA. Entrepreneur. Jewish Peoplehood enthusiast. Founder of שזור/Interwoven. Director of the Z3 Project, an initiative of the Oshman Family JCC.

Rabbi Jason Fruithandler is the rabbi at Woodbury Jewish Center, a Conservative congregation found on the north shore of Long Island. He was ordained by the Jewish Theological Seminary of America in 2011. He also served as an associate rabbi at Sinai Temple in Los Angeles from 2011-2018.

Melanie Roth Gorelick is the Senior Vice President of the Jewish Council for Public Affairs (JCPA). Her portfolio includes overseeing the JCPA programming and conferences, domestic and international policy, communications, leadership, and grassroots organizing work of the JCPA and DC engagement and outreach. She also organizes the JCPA Leadership Mission to Israel. Melanie has received the Essex County Stars Award in 2012 from Essex County Celebrates Jewish Heritage Month, JCPA Program Excellence Award, 2014, Outstanding Human Rights Community Activist 2014 from the Human Rights Institute at Kean University, and JFNA Government Affairs Professional of the Year award in 2015 and the 2018 Founder Liberator Award from the NJ Coalition Against Human Trafficking. Her prior experience includes working as the Communications and Advocacy Manager at the UN Development Fund for Women (UNIFEM), Associate in the Program and Policy Department of the American Association of University Women (AAUW), and Program Assistant at the UN Non-Governmental Liaison Service.

Rabbi Debra Newman Kamin is the rabbi of Am Yisrael in Northfield, IL and President of the Rabbinical Assembly, the international Organization of Conservative Rabbis.

Julia Knobloch was born and raised in Germany and has lived in France, Portugal, and Argentina. She currently serves as a Planning Executive at UJA-Federation of New York. She is a former documentary filmmaker, a member of the Sweet Action poetry collective, and the recipient of a 2017 Brooklyn Poets Fellowship. Her debut poetry collection Do Not Return was published in 2019 by Broadstone Books.

Rabbi Claudia Kreiman is the rabbi at Temple Beth Zion in Brookline, MA. Rav Claudia grew up in Santiago, Chile, where her father, Rabbi Angel Kreiman-Brill was the Chief Rabbi of Chile. In 1994, Rav Claudia's mother, Susy Wolynski Kreiman, was killed in the Asociación Mutual Israelita Argentina (AMIA) bombing in Buenos Aires, along with 84 other victims. The death of Rav Claudia's mother in the attack was one of the most traumatic and shocking experiences of her life. Her mother, Susy was a committed teacher and social work, and inspired Rav Claudia to honor her legacy by committing herself to Jewish education. She is a member of the JStreet Rabbinic Cabinet, of the Brookline Clergy Association, and is involved with Truah: The Rabbinic Call for Human Rights, and is one of the "tomato rabbis", engendering the call for fair wages and safe working conditions for all people, including farmworkers.

Rabbi David Evan Markus is North America's only active pulpit rabbi simultaneously holding a full-time government role. In spiritual life, he serves as rabbi of Temple Beth El of City Island, senior builder for Bayit: Building Jewish (spiritual innovation incubator), rabbinics faculty at the Academy for Jewish Religion, spiritual direction faculty for ALEPH, and trustee of the Center of Theological Inquiry at Princeton Theological Seminary. In secular life, he presides in New York Supreme Court in a parallel public service career that has spanned all branches and levels of government. He earned double ordination as rabbi and mashpia ruchani (spiritual director) from ALEPH, a graduate certificate in spiritual entrepreneurship from the Columbia Business School executive MBA partnership with CLAL, a Juris Doctor from Harvard Law School, a Masters in Public Policy from Harvard University's John F. Kennedy School of Government, and a Bachelor of Arts from Williams College. He lives in New York.

Rabbi Jack Moline is president of Interfaith Alliance (interfaithalliance.org) and Rabbi Emeritus of Agudas Achim Congregation in Alexandria, VA.

Sarah Rudolph is a Jewish educator and freelance writer. She has been sharing her passion for Jewish texts of all kinds for 20 years, with students of all ages. Sarah's essays have been published in a variety of internet and print media, including Times of Israel, Kveller, Jewish Action, 929 English, Lehrhaus, and more. Sarah lives in Ohio with her husband and four children, but is privileged to learn online with students all over the world.

Rabbi Annie Tucker is the senior rabbi of Temple Israel Center in White Plains, NY. Her leadership has extended communal commitments to adult learning, inclusion, interfaith efforts, LGBTQ inclusion and social justice efforts—including helping to launch a relief mission to Houston after Hurricane Harvey.

Ruth Zakarin spent over 20 years working with survivors of domestic and sexual violence, as well as human trafficking. In May of 2019, Ruth became the Executive Director of the Massachusetts Coalition to Prevent Gun Violence, which includes over 90 member organizations working in collaboration to address gun violence in our communities. Ruth has particular interest in raising awareness about the intersection of domestic violence and guns, and in engaging youth voices to shape the conversation about community violence. She is passionate about prevention, community organizing, knitting, and coffee. She is the very proud mom of two fabulous teenagers, who are fast developing into our next generation of leaders.

Made in the USA
Middletown, DE
29 January 2020